Common Core
Women's Su

By

MW00945589

Published by Gallopade International, Inc.
©Carole Marsh/Gallopade
Printed in the U.S.A. (Peachtree City, Georgia)

TABLE OF CONTENTS

G: Includes Graphic Organizer
GO: Graphic Organizer is also available 8½" x 11" online
download at www.gallopade.com/client/go
(numbers above correspond to the graphic organizer numbers online)

Seneca Falls Convention

Read the text and answer the questions.

The women's suffrage movement began in 1840 with a small conversation between Elizabeth Cady Stanton and Lucretia Mott. They met at an anti-slavery <u>convention</u> in London that refused to seat female delegates. Stanton and Mott privately discussed wanting a convention to address the problem of women's rights.

In 1848, a social gathering brought together Elizabeth Stanton, Lucretia Mott, Martha Wright, Mary Ann McClintock, and Jane Hunt. All five women were familiar with anti-slavery and temperance conventions, and four women were Quakers. Together, they decided to organize the Seneca Falls Convention to discuss the "social, civil, and religious condition and rights of woman."

Stanton wrote the Declaration of Sentiments and modeled it after the Declaration of Independence. She changed the words to say that, "all men and women are created equal." She also included eleven resolutions to be discussed at the convention and a list of injuries "on the part of man toward woman."

The women held the Seneca Falls Convention on July 19 and 20, 1948. Over 300 people attended, including 40 men, one of which was the abolitionist Frederick Douglass. At the convention, the men and women voted on several resolutions presented by Stanton's Declaration of Sentiments. All of the resolutions were quickly passed, except women's suffrage—the right to vote. Elizabeth Cady Stanton argued, "I saw clearly that the power to make the laws was the right through which all other rights could be secured." Frederick Douglass eventually convinced the convention to pass Stanton's voting resolution. Although no laws were changed, the Seneca Falls Convention was the first organized movement toward women's suffrage in America.

1. What event prompted Stanton and Mott to discuss the need for a women's rights convention?

2. Describe the character and beliefs of the women who organized the Seneca Falls Convention by making inferences from the text.

3. What right is Stanton supporting when she says "the power to make the laws?" Do you agree or disagree with her claim? Explain.

Woman Suffrage Organizations

In 1869, members of the American Equal Rights Association (AERA) disagreed on whether or not to support the 15th Amendment. Therefore, the AERA divided into the National Woman Suffrage Association (NWSA) and the American Woman Suffrage Association (AWSA). However, in 1890, the two organizations merged into the National American Woman Suffrage Association (NAWSA) to support a common goal.

Use an online resource to complete the flowchart.

National Woman Suffrage Association (1869)

Leaders:

Methods:

American Woman Suffrage Association (1869)

Leaders:

Methods:

Common Goal

National American Woman Suffrage Association (1890)

Leaders:

Methods:

Declarations Comparison

Read the documents and answer the questions.

Declaration of Independence (excerpt)
IN CONGRESS, July 4, 1776

1)   When in the Course of human events, it becomes necessary for one people to <u>dissolve the political bands which have connected them with another</u>, and to assume among the powers of the earth, the separate and equal station to which the Laws of Nature and of Nature's God entitle them...

2)   We hold these truths to be self-evident, that all men are created equal, that they are endowed by their Creator with certain unalienable Rights, that among these are Life, Liberty and the pursuit of Happiness...--That whenever any Form of Government becomes destructive of these ends, it is the Right of the People to alter or to abolish it... The history of the present King of Great Britain is a history of repeated injuries and usurpations, all having in direct object the establishment of an absolute Tyranny over these States. To prove this, let Facts be submitted to a candid world.

3)   He has refused his Assent to Laws, the most wholesome and necessary for the public good...

4)   He has dissolved Representative Houses repeatedly, for opposing with manly firmness his invasions on the rights of the people...

5)   He has plundered our seas, ravaged our Coasts, burnt our towns, and destroyed the lives of our people...

---

1. What is the purpose of each document? Explain.

2. What can you infer about the relationship between these two documents? Cite evidence to support your answer.

3. What is meant by <u>dissolve</u> in the Declaration of Independence? Why is that word not included in the Declaration of Sentiments?

4. What is the most important difference between section 2 of the Declaration of Independence and section 2 of the Declaration of Sentiments from the perspective of a suffragist?

Declaration of Sentiments (excerpt)
Seneca Falls Convention, 1948
prepared by Elizabeth Cady Stanton

1)   When, in the course of human events, it becomes necessary for one portion of the family of man to assume among the people of the earth a position different from that which they have hitherto occupied, but one to which the laws of nature and of nature's God entitle them...

2)   We hold these truths to be self-evident: that all men and women are created equal; that they are endowed by their Creator with certain inalienable rights; that among these are life, liberty, and the pursuit of happiness...Whenever any form of government becomes destructive of these ends, it is the right of those who suffer from it to refuse allegiance to it... But when a long train of abuses and usurpations, pursuing invariably the same object evinces a design to reduce them under absolute despotism, it is their duty to throw off such government...

3)   The history of mankind is a history of repeated injuries and usurpations on the part of man toward woman, having in direct object the establishment of an absolute tyranny over her. To prove this, let facts be submitted to a candid world.

4)   He has compelled her to submit to laws, in the formation of which she had no voice...

5)   He has made her, if married, in the eye of the law, civilly dead...

6)   He has taken from her all right in property, even to the wages she earns...

---

5.   What problem is stated in section 4 of the Declaration of Sentiments? What solution did Stanton propose?

6.   What is the purpose of Sections 4-6 of the Declaration of Sentiments?

7.   To whom is "he" referring in the Declaration of Independence? To whom is "he" referring in the Declaration of Sentiments?

8.   In a well-organized essay, react to the following quotation. Do you agree or disagree? Defend your point of view with examples.

   "The history of mankind is a history of repeated injuries and usurpations on the part of man toward woman..."

Mothers of the Movement

Read the text and answer the questions.

> ### House Resolution 391 (excerpt)
> September 7, 2000
>
> Recognizing the contributions of Susan B. Anthony and Elizabeth Cady Stanton to the women's suffrage;
>
> Whereas in 1866, Susan B. Anthony and Elizabeth Cady Stanton together formed the American Equal Rights Association, dedicated to securing the ballot for African American men and all women;

Stanton (left) Anthony (right)

> Whereas in 1869 Susan B. Anthony and Elizabeth Cady Stanton formed the National Woman Suffrage Association, a woman-led organization devoted to obtaining a federal women's suffrage constitutional amendment;
>
> Whereas although neither Susan B. Anthony nor Elizabeth Cady Stanton lived to see the day when women were allowed to vote, their relentless years of work should not be forgotten... therefore, be it resolved by the House of Representatives (the Senate concurring), that the Congress --
>
> 1)   Encourages all Americans to remember the contributions of Susan B. Anthony and Elizabeth Cady Stanton to women's suffrage; and
>
> 2)   Urges the President to issue a proclamation calling on the people of the United States to conduct appropriate ceremonies, activities, and programs to commemorate the women's suffrage movement.

1. What is the purpose of House Resolution 391?

2. What two organizations were established by Susan B. Anthony and Elizabeth Cady Stanton? Explain the purpose of each organization.

3. What inferences can you make from the photograph?

4. Why should we remember the women's suffrage movement today?

PRIMARY SOURCE ANALYSIS

"Ain't I a Woman?"

Read the text and answer the questions.

"Ain't I a Woman?" speech by Sojourner Truth (excerpt)
Recalled by: Frances Dana Barker Gage
Printed in the <u>History of Woman Suffrage</u> in May 1863

Well, children, where there is so much racket there must be something out of kilter. I think that 'twixt the negroes of the South and the women at the North, all talking about rights, the white men will be in a fix pretty soon. But what's all this here talking about?

That man over there says that women need to be helped into carriages, and lifted over ditches, and to have the best place everywhere. Nobody ever helps me into carriages, or over mud-puddles, or gives me any best place! And ain't I a woman? Look at me! Look at my arm! I have ploughed and planted, and gathered into barns, and no man could head me! And ain't I a woman? I could work as much and eat as much as a man—when I could get it—and bear the lash as well! And ain't I a woman? I have borne thirteen children, and seen most all sold off to slavery, and when I cried out with my mother's grief, none but Jesus heard me! And ain't I a woman?

Then they talk about this thing in the head; what's this they call it? [member of audience whispers, "intellect"] That's it, honey. What's that got to do with women's rights or negroes' rights? If my cup won't hold but a pint, and yours holds a quart, wouldn't you be mean not to let me have my little half measure full?

1. Use the text to make 3-5 inferences about Sojourner Truth.

2. Describe the tone and style of this speech. Cite examples.

3. Why did Sojourner Truth give this speech?

4. Explain the difference between the speaker and the author of the text.

5. What point is Sojourner Truth making by repeating the phrase, "Ain't I a woman?"

6. Sojourner Truth uses colloquial language in her speech. Analyze the text and explain what is meant by "racket," "cup," "my little half measure full," and other expressive phrases. Discuss as a class.

National Woman's Party

Read the text and answer the questions.

The National Woman's Party began with Alice Paul and Lucy Burns. While participating in the British women's suffrage movement, the two American women confronted police authorities, endured jail sentences, and participated in hunger strikes. Paul and Burns returned to America and used similar <u>tactics</u> to energize the American women's suffrage movement.

In 1913, Alice Paul and Lucy Burns organized the National American Woman Suffrage Association (NAWSA) parade on Washington D.C. on March 3—the day before President Woodrow Wilson's inauguration. Bands, floats, and over 8,000 marchers participated. The march successfully warned the President, Congress, and the public that the United States could not ignore the women's suffrage movement forever.

In late 1913, Alice Paul and Lucy Burns separated from NAWSA. They created the Congressional Union for Woman Suffrage (CU). The CU continued to use the British-inspired tactics and became the National Woman's Party (NWP) in 1916.

The NWP organized local, state, and federal movements to support women's suffrage. They picketed conventions, placed advertisements, and distributed pamphlets. In 1917, the NWP became the first group to picket in front of the White House. Many people were arrested, but the group's continued efforts during WWI helped convince President Woodrow Wilson to support the 19th Amendment, which guaranteed women's suffrage.

1. Use the text to write a definition for <u>tactics</u>.

2. What is meant by the phrase "energize the American women's suffrage movement" in the first paragraph?

3. Explain how the British women's suffrage movement influenced the actions of Alice Paul and Lucy Burns.

4. What was the result of the parade on Washington?

5. What role did the National Women's Party play in gaining women's suffrage?

Suffragist Tactics

Use an online resource to research women's suffragist tactics and complete the graphic organizer. Then answer the questions.

Lobbying

Imprisonment

Purpose:

_____

Parades

_____

Purpose:

Example:

Purpose:

Example:

Example:

SUFFRAGIST TACTICS

Pagaents

Picketing

Purpose:

Example:

Purpose:

Example:

1. How are the purposes of the tactics similar? How are they different?

2. A. In small groups, use an online resource to research one specific tactic of the women's suffrage movement. Create a slideshow presentation explaining the who, what, when, where, and why of your specific tactic. Include pictures and examples of your tactic. What results did your tactic achieve?

   B. Present your slideshow and discuss as a class.

SUMMARIZING INFORMATION

Suffrage Quotes

Explain each quotation to complete the chart. Use the completed chart to answer the questions.

Quotations:	What it means:
1) "I declare to you that woman must not depend on the protection of man, but must be taught to protect herself, and there I take my stand."	
2) "Come, come, my conservative friend, wipe the dew off your spectacles, and see that the world is moving."	
3) "Women are not suffering any injustice which giving them the ballot would <u>rectify</u>."	
4) "Man's service to the State through government is <u>counter-balanced</u> by woman's service in the Home. One service is just as essential to the welfare of the State as the other, but they can never be identical"	

1. Write a quotation expressing the opposite point of view from quote 1.

2. Describe the tone of quote 2.

3. What is meant by the term <u>rectify</u> in quote 3?

4. What is meant by the term <u>counter-balanced</u> in quote 4?

5. A. Which quotations express the point of view of a suffragist?
    B. Which quotations express the point of view of an anti-suffragist?

Suffrage Vocabulary

Use a dictionary and other resources to complete the graphic organizer for each vocabulary word.

amendment   petition   suffrage

citizenship   picket   suffragist

convention   ratify   temperance

declaration   rights

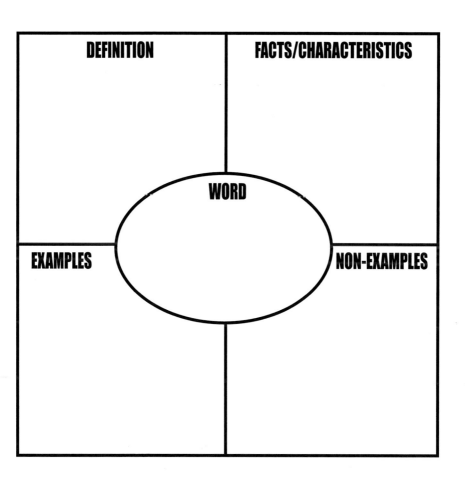

Women's Suffrage

Summarize key information about the women's suffrage movement to complete the graphic organizer. List and explain the movement's key Beliefs and Goals. Then identify the People, Methods and Events and describe the achieved Results.

"We hold these truths..."

Beliefs and Goals

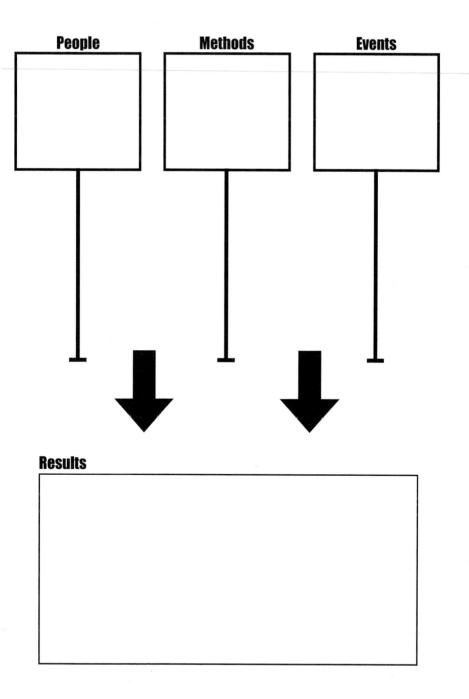

People

Methods

Events

Results

Women's Roles During WWI

Read the text and answer the questions.

Many men joined the military when World War I began in 1914. As a result, it quickly became clear that women were needed in the workforce—not only in the home as before. Working women found new freedom in jobs usually held by men. Women primarily filled roles in government departments, public transportation, post offices, and secretarial positions. Women also contributed to the war effort by working in dangerous ammunition factories to produce shells and weapons for the British and U.S. militaries.

Women filled an important role in the military, too. Many women became medical nurses, and others were trained as clerks, phone operators, and stenographers. Besides paid jobs, women took on the responsibility of voluntary work as well. They rolled bandages, knitted clothing, and prepared supplies for men on the war front.

Approximately 1,600,000 women joined the workforce during WWI. Their activity proved that women could do men's work, women could hold responsibility, and women were necessary to victory in WWI. Women's involvement in WWI made it difficult for politicians to ignore the women's suffrage movement. As a result, women's roles in WWI helped the passage of the 19th Amendment.

1. What was the primary role of women before World War I?

2. During World War I, why did women take on jobs usually held by men?

3. Explain how WWI offered women new opportunites and freedoms.

4. Explain the relationship between women's roles in WWI and the passage of the 19th Amendment.

Writing Prompt:

Imagine you are a woman in America during WWI. What job would you choose to perform? Write a first-hand narrative describing your role in the war effort, at home or in the military, and describe how it is different than your life before. Proofread and edit your work.

"Kaiser Wilson" Propaganda Poster

Look at the photograph and answer the questions.

Courtesy of Library of Congress

1. A. Use a dictionary to write a definition of <u>Kaiser</u>.
   B. What is the purpose of using "Kaiser Wilson" to refer to U.S. President Woodrow Wilson?

2. Do you think this photograph was taken before, during, or after WWI? Explain your answer.

3. What inferences can you make about the person in this photograph? Explain.

4. What is the purpose of the poster? Describe how the poster helps achieve its purpose.

Women's Suffrage Movement

Put the events in chronological order on the graphic organizer.

NAWSA's Parade on Washington	Seneca Falls Convention	NWSA & AWSA are created	15th Amendment is ratified	President Wilson supports 19th Amendment
NAWSA created	14th Amendment is ratified	National Woman's Party is created	WW I begins; women in workforce	19th Amendment ratified

Women's Suffrage Movement Events:

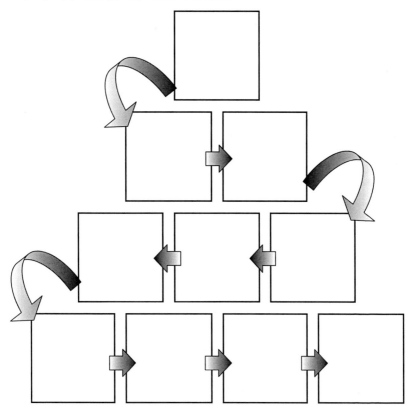

COMPARE AND CONTRAST

Pro vs. Anti-Suffrage

Use the graphic organizer to compare and contrast the points of view of people for and against women's suffrage leading up to the ratification of the 19th Amendment.

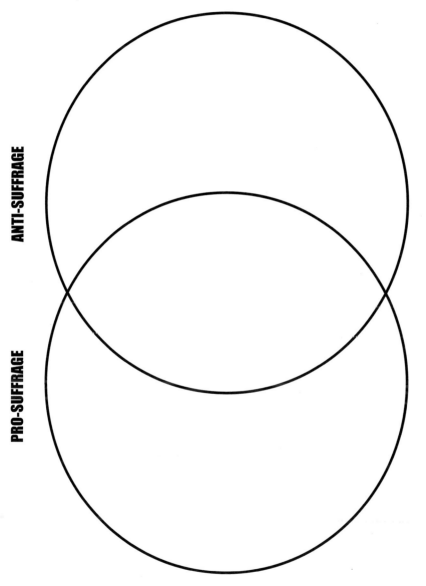

ANTI-SUFFRAGE

PRO-SUFFRAGE

From Convention to 19th Amendment

Complete the graphic organizer by describing the effects of each event of the women's suffrage movement.

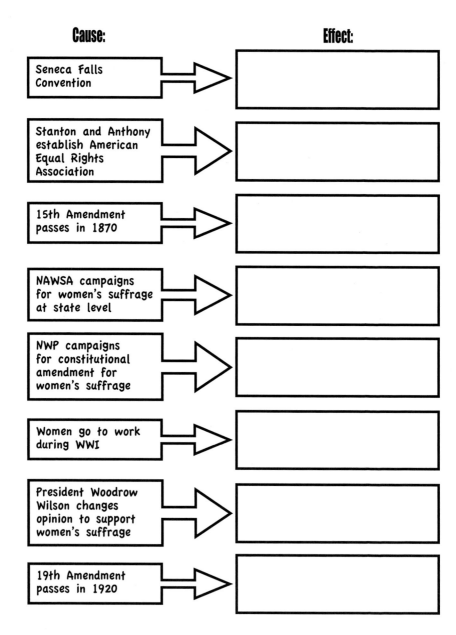

Cause:

Effect:

Seneca Falls Convention →

Stanton and Anthony establish American Equal Rights Association →

15th Amendment passes in 1870 →

NAWSA campaigns for women's suffrage at state level →

NWP campaigns for constitutional amendment for women's suffrage →

Women go to work during WWI →

President Woodrow Wilson changes opinion to support women's suffrage →

19th Amendment passes in 1920 →

Suffrage Cartoon

Analyze the cartoon and answer the questions.

"ALL TOGETHER NOW! STOP HER!"

Courtesy of Library of Congress

1. A. What is represented by the large foot marked with arrow A?
   B. Who is represented by the small people marked with arrow B?

2. What is the message of this cartoon?

3. What symbols and words communicate the message? Explain.

4. Who is the intended audience of this cartoon? Explain.

5. What is the purpose of this cartoon?

6. Discuss the political cartoon as a class. Expand your answers to the previous questions based on new insight and ideas shared.

Women's Suffrage Map in 1920

The map shows the levels of women's suffrage in various states in early August 1920 before the ratification of the 19th Amendment.

Use the map and data to answer the questions.

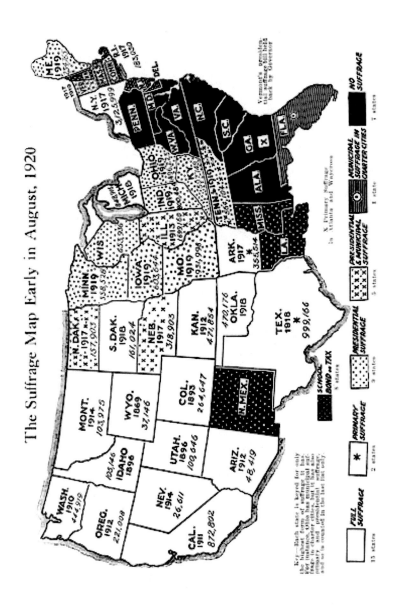

1. _____ In early August 1920, only six states had full suffrage.
2. _____ The majority of Western states had full suffrage before the 19th Amendment.
3. _____ Before 1920, New York's last women's suffrage law was passed in 1919.
4. _____ Florida was the only state in the Southeast in 1920 to have municipal suffrage for women in charter cities.

PART B: Map & Data Skills

5. Which state was the first to have full women's suffrage?
6. According to the map, what level of suffrage did women in Texas have in early August 1920?
7. Explain the difference in suffrage levels between Iowa and Illinois.
8. List the East Coast states that allowed some level of suffrage in 1920.

PART C: Making Inferences

9. What states are not depicted on this map? Why?
10. In what part of the country did women already have the full right to vote before the 19th Amendment?
11. Which part of the country would be mostly against the ratification of the 19th Amendment?
12. Explain why there are no numbers or dates listed on states with no suffrage.
13. The map is drawn according to state suffrage laws before the ratification of the 19th Amendment on August 18, 1920. Explain how the map would change after the ratification of the 19th Amendment.

BONUS: Use the map to explain why an amendment to the U.S. Constitution was necessary to ensure women's suffrage in all states.

The 19ᵗʰ Amendment

Read the text and answer the questions.

The Constitution originally gave states the power to determine who was allowed to vote. In 1875, a woman named Virginia Minor attempted to register to vote in Missouri but was refused. She appealed her case to the Supreme Court in *Minor v. Happersett*. The Supreme Court stated that the 14ᵗʰAmendment includes women as citizens but citizenship did not guarantee women the right to vote.

Before 1900, the majority of states refused women the right to vote. Women's suffrage groups, including the National American Women's Suffrage Association, formed and focused on gaining suffrage in individual states. These groups helped to changed state voting laws and increased women's suffrage in states across the nation. By the early 1910s, many states had passed laws granting women the right to vote. By 1916, most suffrage groups supported the National Women's Party by lobbying Congress, picketing national conventions, and protesting in front of the White House. They demanded a constitutional amendment that would give women in all states the right to vote.

In January 1918, President Wilson publically supported the women's suffrage amendment. Congress approved the 19ᵗʰ Amendment on June 4, 1919. The states ratified the amendment on August 18, 1920.

The 19ᵗʰ Amendment states that, "The right of citizens of the United States to vote shall not be denied or abridged by the United States or any state on account of sex." This amendment overturned the Supreme Court's decision in *Minor v. Happersett* and gave the right to vote to all women citizens in all states.

1. Where did states get their power to deny women the right to vote?

2. What effects did the women's suffrage have on *Minor v. Happersett*?

3. What inferences can you make about the influence of women's suffrage organizations?

4. Why was a constitutional amendment necessary to secure women's suffrage?

Comparing Rights Movements

The women's suffrage movement and the African American civil rights movement were part of a greater movement for overall human rights. Use an online resource to identify key similarities between the women's suffrage movement and the civil rights movement. Include similarities in goals, methods, and events.

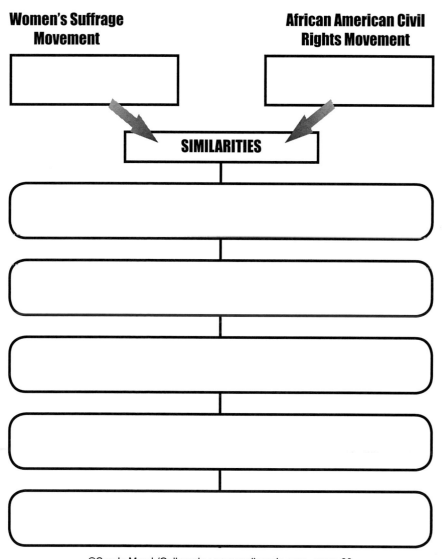

Women's Suffrage Movement

African American Civil Rights Movement

SIMILARITIES

Correlations to Common Core State Standards

For your convenience, correlations are listed page-by-page and for the entire book!

This book is correlated to the Common Core State Standards for English Language Arts grades 3-8, and to Common Core State Standards for Literacy in History, Science, & Technological Subjects grades 6-8.

Correlations are highlighted in gray.

PAGE #	READING	WRITING	LANGUAGE	SPEAKING & LISTENING
	Includes: RI: Reading Informational Text / RH: Reading History	Includes: W: Writing / WHST: Writing History, Science, & Technology	Includes: L: Language / LF: Language Foundational Skills	Includes: SL: Speaking & Listening
2	RI · 1 2 3 4 5 6 7 8 9 10 / RH	W · 1 2 3 4 5 6 7 8 9 10 / WHST	L · 1 2 3 4 5 6 / LF	SL · 1 2 3 4 5 6
3	RI · 1 2 3 4 5 6 7 8 9 10 / RH	W · 1 2 3 4 5 6 7 8 9 10 / WHST	L · 1 2 3 4 5 6 / LF	SL · 1 2 3 4 5 6
4-5	RI · 1 2 3 4 5 6 7 8 9 10 / RH	W · 1 2 3 4 5 6 7 8 9 10 / WHST	L · 1 2 3 4 5 6 / LF	SL · 1 2 3 4 5 6
6	RI · 1 2 3 4 5 6 7 8 9 10 / RH	W · 1 2 3 4 5 6 7 8 9 10 / WHST	L · 1 2 3 4 5 6 / LF	SL · 1 2 3 4 5 6
7	RI · 1 2 3 4 5 6 7 8 9 10 / RH	W · 1 2 3 4 5 6 7 8 9 10 / WHST	L · 1 2 3 4 5 6 / LF	SL · 1 2 3 4 5 6
8	RI · 1 2 3 4 5 6 7 8 9 10 / RH	W · 1 2 3 4 5 6 7 8 9 10 / WHST	L · 1 2 3 4 5 6 / LF	SL · 1 2 3 4 5 6
9	RI · 1 2 3 4 5 6 7 8 9 10 / RH	W · 1 2 3 4 5 6 7 8 9 10 / WHST	L · 1 2 3 4 5 6 / LF	SL · 1 2 3 4 5 6
10	RI · 1 2 3 4 5 6 7 8 9 10 / RH	W · 1 2 3 4 5 6 7 8 9 10 / WHST	L · 1 2 3 4 5 6 / LF	SL · 1 2 3 4 5 6
11	RI · 1 2 3 4 5 6 7 8 9 10 / RH	W · 1 2 3 4 5 6 7 8 9 10 / WHST	L · 1 2 3 4 5 6 / LF	SL · 1 2 3 4 5 6
12-13	RI · 1 2 3 4 5 6 7 8 9 10 / RH	W · 1 2 3 4 5 6 7 8 9 10 / WHST	L · 1 2 3 4 5 6 / LF	SL · 1 2 3 4 5 6
14	RI · 1 2 3 4 5 6 7 8 9 10 / RH	W · 1 2 3 4 5 6 7 8 9 10 / WHST	L · 1 2 3 4 5 6 / LF	SL · 1 2 3 4 5 6
15	RI · 1 2 3 4 5 6 7 8 9 10 / RH	W · 1 2 3 4 5 6 7 8 9 10 / WHST	L · 1 2 3 4 5 6 / LF	SL · 1 2 3 4 5 6
16	RI · 1 2 3 4 5 6 7 8 9 10 / RH	W · 1 2 3 4 5 6 7 8 9 10 / WHST	L · 1 2 3 4 5 6 / LF	SL · 1 2 3 4 5 6
17	RI · 1 2 3 4 5 6 7 8 9 10 / RH	W · 1 2 3 4 5 6 7 8 9 10 / WHST	L · 1 2 3 4 5 6 / LF	SL · 1 2 3 4 5 6
18	RI · 1 2 3 4 5 6 7 8 9 10 / RH	W · 1 2 3 4 5 6 7 8 9 10 / WHST	L · 1 2 3 4 5 6 / LF	SL · 1 2 3 4 5 6
19	RI · 1 2 3 4 5 6 7 8 9 10 / RH	W · 1 2 3 4 5 6 7 8 9 10 / WHST	L · 1 2 3 4 5 6 / LF	SL · 1 2 3 4 5 6
20-21	RI · 1 2 3 4 5 6 7 8 9 10 / RH	W · 1 2 3 4 5 6 7 8 9 10 / WHST	L · 1 2 3 4 5 6 / LF	SL · 1 2 3 4 5 6
22	RI · 1 2 3 4 5 6 7 8 9 10 / RH	W · 1 2 3 4 5 6 7 8 9 10 / WHST	L · 1 2 3 4 5 6 / LF	SL · 1 2 3 4 5 6
23	RI · 1 2 3 4 5 6 7 8 9 10 / RH	W · 1 2 3 4 5 6 7 8 9 10 / WHST	L · 1 2 3 4 5 6 / LF	SL · 1 2 3 4 5 6
COMPLETE BOOK	RI · 1 2 3 4 5 6 7 8 9 10 / RH	W · 1 2 3 4 5 6 7 8 9 10 / WHST	L · 1 2 3 4 5 6 / LF	SL · 1 2 3 4 5 6

For the complete Common Core standard identifier, combine your grade + "." + letter code above + "." + number code above.

In addition to the correlations indicated here, the activities may be adapted or expanded to align to additional standards and to meet the diverse needs of your unique students!

©Carole Marsh/Gallopade • www.gallopade.com • page 24